AMERICAN MUSEUM OF NATURAL HISTORY

INSIDE
BUTTERFLIES

Enter the Wonderful World of Butterflies and Moths

by Hazel Davies

Illustrations throughout by Melisa Beveridge

STERLING CHILDREN'S BOOKS
New York

STERLING CHILDREN'S BOOKS
New York

An Imprint of Sterling Publishing
387 Park Avenue South
New York, NY 10016

Library of Congress Cataloging-in-Publication Data Available

Lot#:
10 9 8 7 6 5 4 3 2 1
04/11
Published by Sterling Publishing Co., Inc.
387 Park Avenue South, New York, NY 10016

www. sterlingpublishing.com/kids

Distributed in Canada by Sterling Publishing
c/o Canadian Manda Group, 165 Dufferin Street
Toronto, Ontario, Canada M6K 3H6
Distributed in the United Kingdom by GMC Distribution Services
Castle Place, 166 High Street, Lewes, East Sussex, England BN7 1XU
Distributed in Australia by Capricorn Link (Australia) Pty. Ltd.
P.O. Box 704, Windsor, NSW 2756, Australia

Sterling ISBN 978-1-4027-7874-2 (hardcover)
          978-1-4027-8161-2 (flexibound)

For information about custom editions, special sales, premium and corporate purchases, please contact Sterling Special Sales Department at 800-805-5489 or specialsales@sterlingpublishing.com.

Series design by Anke Stohlmann Design
Layout by Celia Fuller

For Lisa and Charlie, with love.

Special thanks to Dr. James S. Miller, Melisa Beveridge, Pamela Horn, Ashley Bruhn, and Andrew Davies for their invaluable contributions. Thanks also to David Harvey, Senior Vice President for Exhibition, Dr. David Grimaldi, Suzanne Rab Green, Joseph Sanford, Steve Thurston, Denis Finnin, Rosamond Kinzler, Karen Taber, the Business Development Department and the dedicated staff of Living Exhibits at the American Museum of Natural History. Much gratitude to Ernesto Rodriguez and the staff at El Bosque Nuevo Butterfly Farm, to Dan Dunwoody of Butterfly Dan's, and to Ashley Prine and Celia Fuller at Sterling.

Visit the Museum

The American Museum of Natural History is located in the heart of New York City. One of the world's most respected scientific and cultural institutions, the Museum is renowned for its exhibitions and collections, which serve as a field guide to the entire planet and present a panorama of the world's cultures. Visit the Museum to learn more.

OLogy

The website of the American Museum of Natural History has a special place just for kids. Go to www.amnh.org/ology to do activities, play games, and learn more about butterflies.

THE BEAUTY OF THE BUTTERFLY

You've seen them fluttering near flowers. Their beautiful wings catch your eye. Their graceful movements hold your attention. Butterflies are part of the most diverse group of animals in the world. They are insects, like bees and flies and beetles. They have earned a special place in our world: people plant flowers to attract them to their gardens, and the eye-catching colors and wing-patterns often inspire art.

A group of butterflies called the clearwings have very few scales on their delicate wings, so you can see right through them, just like looking through a window.

Anatomy 101

Like all insects, butterflies and moths have bodies made up of three parts: a head, a *thorax*, and an *abdomen*. All insects have six legs attached to the thorax. Insects do not have an internal skeleton of bones, but instead their body is protected by a tough outer case called an *exoskeleton*. The exoskeleton is made of a substance called *chitin*, the same substance that makes up the shells of crabs and shrimp.

forewing

head

leg

thorax

hindwing

abdomen

spiracle

Butterfly or Moth?

At first glance, it can be difficult to know if you are seeing a butterfly or a moth. People often learn that moths are dull in color and fly at night, while butterflies are brightly colored and fly during the day. This rule is not always true. Many brightly colored moths fly during the day, and some butterflies are dull brown. The best ways to tell them apart are to look at their *antennae*, their body, and the way they hold their wings.

 **Butterfly head**

 **Moth head**

The Madagascan Sunset moth is colorful.

Antenna Alert

If you look closely at the antennae of butterflies and moths, you'll see some clear differences. Butterflies have straight stick-like antennae with a thickened, club-like end. Moth antennae can take all kinds of shapes, but they do not form clubs; most taper to a pointed tip and look like feathers.

 **Resting butterfly**

 **Resting moth**

 **Butterfly**

 **Moth**

Wings at Rest

Butterflies and moths tend to hold their wings in different positions when they are not flying. When resting, butterflies usually hold their wings closed together above their bodies, whereas moths rest with their wings open or folded down over their bodies.

Body Basics

The body of the insect can also give you a clue. Butterflies tend to have smooth-looking, slender abdomens, while moths are generally fatter and often look fuzzy or furry because their bodies are covered with long scales.

CONTENTS

How to Read This Book

This book is different from most you've read. Many of its pages fold out—or flip up! To know where to read next, follow arrows like these ⬆, and look for page numbers to help you find your place. To access more information about butterflies, download Microsoft's free Tag Reader on your smartphone at www.gettag.mobi. Look for tags that look like this ▦ throughout the book. Use your smartphone to take a picture of the tag, which will link to related information, pictures, and videos at the American Museum of Natural History's Web site. If you don't have a smartphone, use the URLs listed in the back of the book. Happy exploring!

BUTTERFLY SENSES

Just like other animals, butterflies and moths use senses to understand the world around them. The senses help them find food and escape from *predators*—other animals that might hunt and eat them. Although they use all five major senses—sight, smell, sound, taste, and touch—in some way, the two main senses used by butterflies and moths are sight and smell.

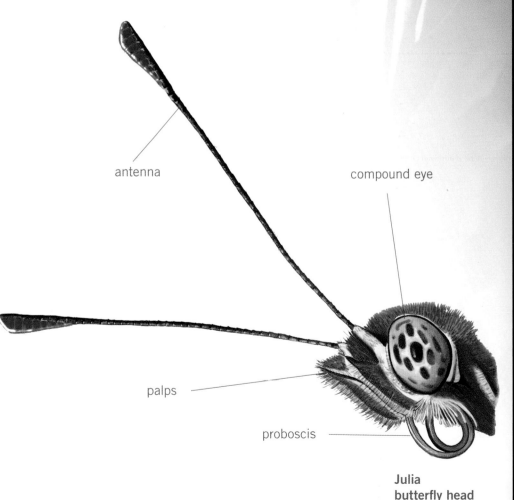

antenna

compound eye

palps

proboscis

Julia butterfly head

Cracker Butterfly

The male Cracker butterfly makes a loud clicking sound with its wings to warn other males away from its territory. Researchers are studying the ears on the butterfly's forewing to understand how it hears the warning.

Sound

Can butterflies and moths hear? Ears can be found on most species of butterflies and moths, but scientists are not sure if they can hear sounds. Scientists have shown that moths flying at night use their ears to detect predators, such as bats. These ears can be located on the forewing, the thorax, or the abdomen.

Touch

Nerve cells attached to special hairs called *tactile setae* relay information about the position of one body part in relation to another, or about something touching the body of the butterfly or moth. The setae are found over most of the insect's body.

A Growing Body

Before becoming a butterfly or moth, the previous stage of the insect's life is in the form of a caterpillar. The caterpillar hatches from an egg, and then spends its time eating and growing until it is time for it to form a *chrysalis* or *cocoon* and then become an adult. (You can see all the stages of its life on page 12.)

Like butterflies or moths, caterpillars come in many different colors and patterns. They are sometimes smooth and sometimes hairy or spiny. But they all have the same basic body structure, made up of a head and 13 body segments.

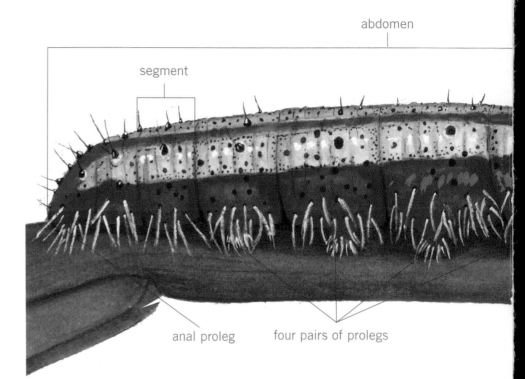

abdomen

segment

anal proleg   four pairs of prolegs

Blue Morpho chrysalis

Monarch chrysalis

Paper Kite chrysalis

Atlas moth cocoons

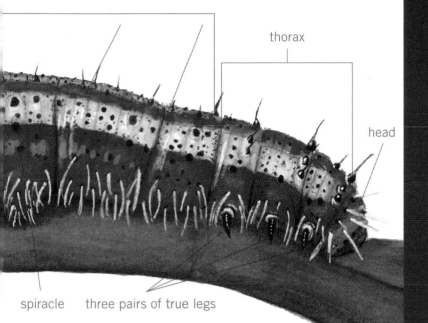

thorax

head

spiracle   three pairs of true legs

Chrysalis or Cocoon?

A *cocoon* is the protective cover a
moth caterpillar makes before it
turns into a *pupa*. Many, but not all,
moths make cocoons. The cocoon
is spun from silk produced by
the caterpillar; often it includes
bits of leaves or twigs in its
construction. Moths that do
not spin a cocoon often make a
chamber, either inside a plant stem or
underground, where they will be safe during
their transformation. Butterfly caterpillars do
not make cocoons; they make an unprotected
chrysalis, usually hanging it from a leaf or twig.
In the chyrsalis, they develop into butterflies.

Beneath the Surface

Like humans, Lepidoptera use blood to
transport nutrients around their bodies.
Insect blood is called *hemolymph*. Moths and
butterflies do not have veins or arteries; the
hemolymph fills the body and is moved around
by a tube-shaped heart.

Unlike humans, Lepidoptera do not have
lungs to help them breathe. They have holes in
their exoskeleton called *spiracles*, which allow
air to move into the body. The spiracles look
like tiny pores along the side of the thorax and
abdomen; they connect to tubes inside that
help move oxygen around the body.

Unlike humans, Lepidoptera do not
maintain a constant body temperature.
Instead, butterflies and moths are ectothermic,
which means they use the outside environment
to control their body temperature. To warm
up, butterflies bask in a sunny spot with their
wings outstretched. At night, moths appear
to shiver, but they are vibrating their flight
muscles to create heat. The long scales on
their body trap the heat inside.

**Basking Lime
Swallowtail**

Butterflies and moths are insects. All insects (animals with a three-part body and six legs) belong to the large group, or class, Insecta. The class Insecta is further sorted into smaller groups called orders. Butterflies and moths belong to the order Lepidoptera.

Within the order Lepidoptera, butterflies and moths are divided into families (which are divided into genera, which are divided into species). Types of moths far outnumber butterflies—one hundred and twenty families of moths to six families of butterflies. In fact, there are approximately 250,000 different species of Lepidoptera alive today, but only 18,000 to 20,000 are butterflies.

Q: What sets Lepidoptera apart from other insects?
A: The tiny scales they have on their wings.

Owl butterfly's scales magnified 100×

Moth scales viewed through a scanning electron microscope (SEM)

Butterflies' and moths' wings are covered in thousands of tiny scales, which make up different wing patterns. Each scale is only one color. The color may come from pigment in a scale, or it may be caused by the way a scale reflects light, giving it a shiny, iridescent look.

The Tailed Jay butterfly has large compound eyes

SEM of a moth's compound eyes

Sight

The eyes of butterflies and moths are made up of thousands of individual eye units called ommatidia. Each *ommatidium* receives light from a small part of the insect's field of vision. Together they form a *compound eye*. Insects' eyes do not focus clearly like ours do but have a wide view and detect motion very well. Butterflies and moths can also see more colors than we can. If you've ever tried to catch a butterfly or another insect with compound eyes, you might have guessed that they can see in all directions without turning their heads.

The feathery antennae of the African Moon moth

Smell

Butterflies and moths do not have noses, but they can smell using scent receptors located on their antennae. A sense of smell is especially important to moths for locating food and mates at night. It is so powerful that some male moths can detect the scent, or *pheromone*, of a female moth from more than a mile away.

An Owl butterfly tastes a banana

Taste

Moths and butterflies have taste receptors located on their feet and on the tip of the *proboscis*, or drinking straw.

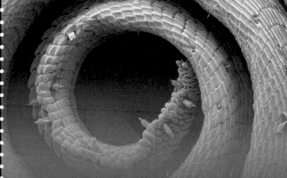
SEM of a proboscis

HOW THE PROBOSCIS WORKS

When an adult butterfly first emerges from its chrysalis, its proboscis is in two separate pieces. The butterfly has to twist and rub the two halves together until the tiny hooks and fringes along the edges join (like Velcro) to make one hollow straw. When not being used, the proboscis is coiled up like a garden hose and tucked away between two protective structures called palps. To feed, the butterfly unrolls its proboscis and the liquid moves up the drinking straw in a process called capillary action, in much the same way that a paper towel absorbs liquid.

Orange-barred Sulphur drinking nectar

Mating Green Birdwings

The main job of an adult butterfly or moth is to reproduce. Like most creatures, in order to reproduce, they must attract a mate. Butterflies and moths use a scent called a pheromone to attract or locate a mate. In butterflies, usually the male emits the pheromones—in moths, it is usually the female. When the male and female find each other, they may fly together in elaborate courtship "dances."

To mate, the male and female join together at the tip of the abdomen. The male uses tiny claspers to hold onto the female while he inserts sperm packets to fertilize her eggs. The mating pair may stay joined together for an hour or more. If they are disturbed, one can take flight, carrying the other below.

A Promethea moth laying eggs

Laying an Egg

After mating, a female will look for suitable places to lay her eggs. Often she will scratch at a leaf with her foot and taste it to make sure it is the correct food for developing caterpillars. Eggs may be laid on the underside of leaves, around stems, on flower buds, or may be released on the ground in the grass. Depending on the species, a butterfly or moth may lay up to 1,000 eggs. Some species lay their eggs one at time, flying from leaf to leaf, while others lay clumps of many eggs in one location.

Eggs of the Great Southern White butterfly

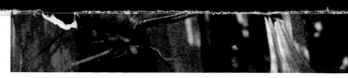

Female Monarch

Male Monarch

Males and Females

In some butterflies, the male and female look completely different; this is called *sexual dimorphism*. In these cases, the male is generally more brightly colored, but the female is often larger. Sometimes the difference is small, and you must look closely to spot it.

Female Shoemaker

Male Shoemaker

FROM CATERPILLAR TO BUTTERFLY

Fourth instar larva

Third instar larva

Lepidoptera don't start off as the beautiful creatures we know. It takes a lot of growing and changing to go from a tiny egg to a wriggling caterpillar to a full-grown flying adult. Few animals go through such distinct stages during their life cycle. In fact, this change has a special name. It is known as complete *metamorphosis*. Metamorphosis of butterflies and moths takes place over the course of four distinct life stages.

Blue Morpho eggs

Second instar larva

First instar larva

1. The Egg

During the first stage, the caterpillar develops inside an egg about the size of a pinhead. It takes three to seven days for the egg to hatch and then the baby caterpillar wriggles out.

2. The Larval Stage

The second part of a butterfly's or moth's life, called the larval stage, begins when it hatches from its egg. This stage is the growing period of the animal's life. The caterpillar eats and eats and grows and grows, starting with its very first meal: the empty eggshell from which it hatched. A caterpillar grows by *molting*, or shedding, its exoskeleton. The old tight skin splits to reveal a new, looser skin underneath that the caterpillar can grow into. Each period of growth is called an *instar*. A caterpillar usually goes through four or five instars as it develops. Often the caterpillar grows more than 3,000 times its weight from when it hatches to when it changes into an adult.

Is It a Caterpillar or a Larva?

It's both! *Caterpillar* is the name we give to the larval stage of a butterfly or moth.

DESIGNED FOR DEFENSE

Lepidoptera are vulnerable to predators at all stages in their life cycle. Both caterpillars and adults make a tasty snack for birds, bats, rodents, and reptiles. Eggs and caterpillars can also fall prey to small parasitic wasps and flies. And, the eggs and caterpillars can catch diseases. To increase their chances of survival, butterflies and moths have evolved in several ways to protect themselves.

Polyphemus moth

Silky Owl

Peacock

Speckled Emperor moth

Eye Spy

Spots on the wings that look like eyes may scare away predators. They can help the insect escape by distracting would-be attackers or by directing a bird to peck at the false eye and not at the vulnerable body.

In Bad Taste

Monarch caterpillars eat toxic milkweed plants. Both the larva and adult taste bad to predators and can even make them sick.

Many species of butterflies do not need to hide from potential predators; they have toxins in their body that make them taste really awful. Some caterpillars have evolved to eat poisonous plants and store the chemicals in their bodies through metamorphosis and into adulthood. Toxic caterpillars are usually boldly marked with bright stripes or spots. The butterflies are usually brightly colored (often orange, pink, or red), or they have strongly contrasting colors (such as black and white) which warn predators to avoid them.

Butterflies and moths, like the Lacewing, drink rainwater or dew droplets to stay hydrated.

When they mate male butterflies, like the Common Grass-yellow, pass minerals to females and need to replace these nutrients before they can mate again. They do this by drinking from damp patches on the ground to obtain the salts dissolved in the water. This is called puddling.

A group of tropical butterflies called the Longwings, found mainly in South and Central America, are able to digest amino acids and protein from pollen. This gives them longer life spans than many other species of adult butterflies—up to six months. The butterfly collects pollen grains on the outside of its proboscis, secretes an enzyme to dissolve the pollen, and then sips the nutrient-rich liquid.

Droppings left behind by mammals are full of nutrition for species like the Common Nawab.

A few species of moths have a sharp-tipped proboscis that can pierce citrus rind and even skin. Vampire moths have a barbed proboscis and sip blood from cattle and other large mammals.

Some moths in Asia drink tears or eye secretions from large mammals such as water buffalo and elephants.

Many species, like the Owl butterflies of Central and South America, sip fruit juices. Because the butterfly's proboscis cannot pierce fruit skin, the butterflies look for rotting fruit that has fallen to the ground.

What's on the Menu?

Not all caterpillars feed on leaves. The caterpillars of more than 99 percent of all butterflies and moths are plant eaters, or *herbivores*, but a few species are meat eaters, or *carnivores*. The caterpillars of Harvester butterflies prey on tiny insects called woolly aphids. Researchers in Hawaii have discovered four moth species that eat snails. And some butterfly caterpillars dine on ant larvae.

Larvae of the Carpenter Worm moth feed on wood. They construct large tunnels through the bark and into the wood of several types of tree, including oak. The larvae grow slowly on the wood diet and can take two to four years to complete their life cycle. They do such damage to trees grown for lumber that the larvae are considered an agricultural pest.

The larvae of clothes moths feed on natural fibers. They can be real pests as they munch holes in wool, felt, silk, and fur—causing damage to clothing, blankets, and floor coverings.

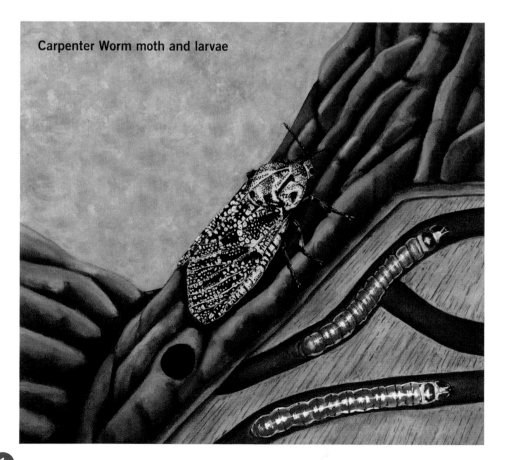

Carpenter Worm moth and larvae

Morgan's Sphinx moth

Grown-up Food

Because they don't have jaws for chewing, butterflies and moths use a proboscis. The length of the proboscis is different for each species. Generally, smaller species have a shorter proboscis, but that also varies, depending on the insect's preferred diet. Those that drink *nectar*—a sugar-rich liquid from flowers—tend to have a longer, thinner proboscis than species that drink fruit juice or other liquids. The record for the longest proboscis, at 10 inches (25 cm), belongs to the Morgan's Sphinx moth from Africa, which drinks from long tubelike orchid blooms.

TIME TO EAT

The way butterflies and moths eat at each stage in their life cycle is very different. Caterpillars are munching machines, with strong jaws designed to chew on plant material such as leaves, stems, or roots. Adults, on the other hand, do not have chewing mouthparts. Instead they have a flexible drinking straw, called a proboscis, which they use to drink liquids.

Did You Know?

Some species of moths have no mouthparts at all and never eat or drink as adults.

The Luna Moth has no mouthparts

Question Mark caterpillar

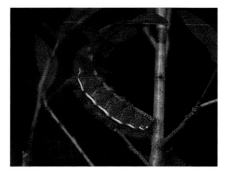

Io moth caterpillar

Caterpillar Crunching

Most caterpillars feed on plant material, and many species eat only one type of plant—known as their *hostplant*. The Monarch caterpillar, for example, can only feed on the leaves of milkweed plants. Other species can eat a variety of different plants. The Question Mark caterpillar feeds on the leaves of many types of trees. Sometimes the larvae of a species will eat different hostplants, depending on where they live. An example is the Io moth in North America.

Bird droppings
are a good source
of nourishment.
They provide
essential salts
for Lepidoptera,
such as the Red
Admiral.

Sugary, sticky
tree sap is a
favorite food for
species such as
the Mourning
Cloak.

Perspiration and
urine contain
valuable dissolved
salts and minerals.
Butterflies, like the
Purple Emperor,
will drink from
moist urine spots
left by other
animals and will
perch on a sweaty
animal—including
a human—to sip
the perspiration.

Some butterflies, like the Question Mark, visit decaying animal carcasses to feed.

The main diet of most butterflies and moths, including the Zebra Swallowtail, is flower nectar, which consists mainly of water and sugar. Some species of butterflies and moths specialize in feeding from flowers of only one color.

The Harvester butterfly has a very short proboscis and feeds on honeydew, a sweet excretion produced by woolly aphids.

The fully grown larva prepares to shed its skin for the final time and reveal the chrysalis

Newly formed chrysalis

As the butterfly is close to emerging, the chrysalis becomes darker

3. The Pupal Stage

The caterpillar eventually forms a chrysalis or cocoon, inside of which dramatic changes occur. During this period of the life cycle, known as the pupal stage, the body of the caterpillar breaks down, and its cells are rearranged to form the structure of an adult.

Word Power

Meta = change
Morph = form
Metamorphosis = change in form

4. Adult

In the final stage in the life cycle, the adult emerges from the chrysalis or cocoon—in a process called *eclosion*. Before it can fly away, the new butterfly or moth must wait for its wings to straighten out and dry. Adult butterflies live from about two weeks to several months, depending on the species. Adult moths live from several days to over a year.

The newly emerged butterfly hangs to expand and dry its wings

A beautiful Blue Morpho butterfly

15

CRAZY FOR CAMOUFLAGE

Many species of butterflies and moths have evolved to blend in with their surroundings. They match the colors and patterns of leaves, tree bark, moss, or rocks, which is called *cryptic coloration*, or *camouflage*.

The Indian Leafwing butterfly probably has the best camouflage of all, because it looks exactly like a leaf, right down to having a tail that looks like a stem.

Pipevine Swallowtail butterfly caterpillar, rearing up in a defensive posture and exposing the osmeterium. (Approximately 10× actual size)

Larvae of the Julia butterfly are not only toxic, but also are covered in protective spines. (Approximately 6× actual size)

How Irritating!

To avoid being eaten, some caterpillars are covered in irritating hairs or spines attached to poison sacs that cause a nasty rash for anyone who handles them. Others regurgitate food or emit nasty smells in an effort to scare off predators. Swallowtail larvae have a pair of brightly colored, fleshy horns, called an *osmeterium*, which pop up from behind the head and give off a pungent smell when the caterpillars sense danger.

Word Power

Aposematism: Having bright warning colors to tell predators that you taste really bad or are poisonous.

Batesian
Mimicry

Pipevine Swallowtail (model)

Red-spotted Purple (mimic)

**Female Eastern Tiger
Swallowtail (mimic)**

Mimicry

• • • • • • • • • • • • • • • • • •

Some perfectly tasty butterflies have evolved an effective plan to avoid becoming lunch. Using *mimicry*, the butterfly copies the colors, patterns, and behavior of toxic species that predators have learned to avoid. The species that is being copied is called the model; the one copying it is called the mimic. Some butterflies and moths mimic a completely different insect altogether.

Hornet moth

There are two types of mimicry: When a non-toxic species (mimic) copies the wing patterns of a toxic species (model), it is called Batesian mimicry, after Henry Walter Bates, who first described the process in 1862. The nontoxic species often emerges from the chrysalis later in the season than its toxic model, when predators have already learned to avoid the color pattern of the toxic species.

Because predators learn that certain colors and patterns should be avoided, some toxic species have evolved to look very similar to one another, so that predators learn more quickly to avoid them. This is called Müllerian mimicry, after Fritz Müller, who described it in 1878. All the species benefit from looking alike, so fewer individuals are eaten. (Safety in numbers!)

Mullerian
Mimicry

Harmonia Tiger (co-mimic)

Isabella Tiger (co-mimic)

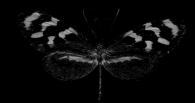

Polymnia Tigerwing (co-mimic)

FRIEND OR FOE?

Butterflies and moths are a very important part of the environment. Adults visiting flowers are second only to bees as essential *pollinators* of many plants. Their larvae and adults are part of the food web, providing nutrition for animals such as birds and bats. Caterpillars break down wood and dead leaves, recycling the nutrients back into the soil. But infestations of caterpillars can eat trees and damage crops, making the caterpillars a potential agricultural pest responsible for millions of dollars in damage.

1. The silkworm larva munches only on mulberry leaves and grows through five instars in less than one month.

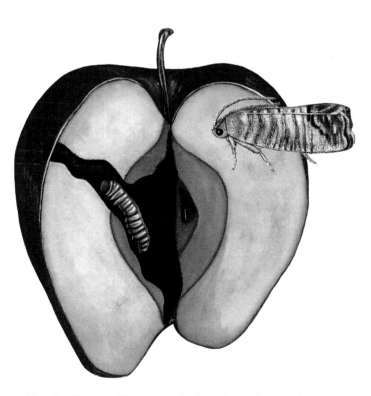

The Codling moth is a pest of apple orchards. As soon as it hatches, the caterpillar burrows into the fruit, eating and spoiling the apples.

Pesky Caterpillars

When caterpillars become so numerous in an agricultural region that they damage crops, they become agricultural pests. Possibly the most costly crop pest in North America is the Corn Earworm. It is also known as the Tomato Fruitworm and Cotton Bollworm. It eats a wide variety of plants, including cotton, asparagus, cabbage, lima beans, spinach, and watermelon, but the larvae prefer corn and tomato. At the same time, the adult moth is a useful pollinator!

Controlling Pests

Controlling infestations of pest caterpillars must be carefully managed so as not to damage the environment and other organisms. Pesticides may be sprayed on plants to kill pests. Sometimes, predatory insects are released into the infested area to damage the eggs and larvae of the pest species. This method is called biological control.

Bagworm moth cocoon, constructed from twigs

Zebra Mosaic chrysalis

Common Mime chrysalis

Thoas Swallowtail chrysalis

Camo for Chrysalides

When a butterfly or moth is in its chrysalis or pupa, it is mostly defenseless. It can't fly or move away from predators so it must do its best to keep predators from seeing it. Most chrysalides are green or brown to blend in with the plants from which they hang. Their shape can resemble leaves and twigs. When moths spin cocoons, they may add leaves and twigs for added camouflage.

The Lesser Purple Emperor larva is well camouflaged on its hostplant.

Cautious Caterpillars

Caterpillars often hide during the day, coming out to eat at night, when they are less likely to be seen by predators. For good measure, many also have well-developed camouflage. For example, some *Swallowtail* caterpillars look exactly like bird droppings on the surface of a leaf; others resemble snakes or look like twigs. Some even roll over the edge of a leaf and secure it around themselves with silk. Other species live together in a large group and spin a silken web, for safety in numbers.

Larva of the Giant Swallowtail

Larva of the Great Mormon Swallowtail

The upper surface of the Question Mark's wings are bright orange, but when the wings are closed the butterfly is well camouflaged.

Now You See Me, Now You Don't

Some butterflies have drab colors on the underside of their wings and bright colors on top. They can blend in very well with their surroundings when resting with their wings closed and the underside showing. If the butterfly is threatened, it can open its wings and startle the attacker with a sudden bold flash of color. Having bright, iridescent colors on the top of the wings and drab, cryptic colors below is also make it difficult for predators to follow a butterfly in flight as it opens and closes its wings.

MIGRATION

Butterflies and moths living in the *tropics* have a fairly stable, predictable climate throughout the year. But those living in other areas often undergo periods of weather that are life-threatening for insects, such as freezing cold temperatures, excessive heat or drought, or stormy rainy seasons. In order to survive, Lepidoptera have evolved ways to live through the harsh conditions.

Beating the Heat

Even in places where it is warm, butterflies may have times when they need to lie low. For example, desert species may have to wait out a period when their food plants are not growing. During this time, they may enter a period of inactivity called *aestivation*. Some species may spend several years waiting in the chrysalis to emerge only when rains trigger plant growth.

Waiting out the Winter

Butterflies and moths must be warm to fly, so low winter temperatures make life difficult. Many species wait out the winter by hibernating. Each species is different; most *hibernate* during the pupal stage, some as eggs or young caterpillars, and a few as adults. During hibernation, the insect's breathing and metabolism slow down, and they do not eat. The arrival of warmer spring weather signals the end of hibernation, and the butterfly or moth will continue its life cycle.

The Small Tortoiseshell in northern Europe hibernates as an adult. It finds shelter under loose bark, or in places such as attics and garages.

Butterfly Navigation

Scientists aren't sure how butterflies find their way, but each year butterflies all over the world migrate hundreds or even thousands of miles. Researchers suggest they may use Earth's magnetic field, the angle of the Sun's rays, or large geographical features such as lakes and rivers to point them in the right direction.

Monarchs west of the Rocky Mountains migrate to sheltered groves along the coast of California to wait out the winter.

Monarchs in eastern North America fly south in the fall, heading to over-wintering sites in Mexico. Some may travel more than 2,500 miles (4,023 km). In the spring, they mate and lay eggs along the way as they return north. Their offspring continue the northward journey.

2. When fully grown, the larva starts to construct a cocoon by secreting silk from a spinneret in its mouth.

3. The larva weaves a silken thread in a figure-eight pattern around itself. It takes between two and three days to form the cocoon.

4. The cocoons are harvested before a moth can emerge, and processed into silk thread.

The Secret of Silk

Farmed caterpillars can provide us with luxurious fabric—silk. The Silkworm moth is entirely domesticated and is raised for the silk cocoons that the caterpillars produce. The white caterpillars, which feed only on mulberry leaves, start spinning cocoons about four weeks after hatching. The caterpillar spins silk in a figure-eight pattern from a single unbroken thread about 3,000 feet (900 meters) long to make its cocoon. To harvest the silk, the cocoons are dipped into warm water to loosen the natural gum, and the delicate, yet strong, thread is wound onto a reel.

Did You Know?

In many parts of the world indigenous people eat caterpillars. They are a good source of protein.

GOING...
GOING...GONE?

Butterflies and moths can be threatened by a variety of factors: Clearing forests, plowing grasslands, and draining wetlands for agriculture and urban development can destroy essential habitat. Spraying pesticides to control other insects, such as mosquitoes, can reduce butterfly populations—as can pollution. Introducing a new species to a butterfly habitat can also crowd out the native animals already living there. While humans are often to blame for a reduction in butterfly populations, many people are now working to make sure Lepidoptera are still around for generations to come.

Clearing the Homerus Swallowtail's natural forest habitat in Jamaica to plant pine trees for timber severely reduced the amount of caterpillar hostplants available for breeding. This butterfly is now an endangered species.

Degree of Concern

Lepidoptera are very sensitive to changes in the environment. Any imbalance or reduction in their habitat can reduce the number of butterflies or moths that can live there. Sometimes a population size falls so low that it is in danger of disappearing forever. A species may be considered vulnerable, threatened, or endangered, depending on the degree of concern for its survival. A species that has completely disappeared is considered *extinct*.

The Queen Alexandra's Birdwing, the largest butterfly in the world, with a wingspan up to 12 inches (30 cm), is only found on the island of Papua New Guinea. It is endangered because its rain forest habitat has been cleared for agriculture. This species is now protected, making it illegal to capture and sell wild specimens.

Painted Lady butterflies are found all over the world. In several places, they go on spectacular migrations. In spring, they leave northern Africa and travel north throughout Europe, looking for food plants and better breeding conditions.

When monsoon rains fall in March and April, a mixed migration of butterflies, including the Dark Blue Tiger and Double Banded Crow, moves across southern India.

Several species of butterflies migrate in East Africa, including the African Emigrant. The migrations are seasonal and are due to periods of rain and food plant availability.

Tropical Hotspot

Butterflies and moths are found on every continent in the world, except Antarctica. They have evolved to live in diverse habitats, from jungles to desert to arctic tundra, but the largest concentration of species lives in the tropics.

In Taiwan, Purple Crow butterflies spend the winter in the island's warmer southern region. Then in spring, the butterflies fly 250 miles (402 km) to their northern *habitats*. At one place in the journey, millions funnel together to cross a major highway—and cause havoc to traffic. More than 10,000 butterflies can cross the highway every minute!

In Australia, Bogong moths fly south each spring from the lowlands of Queensland and New South Wales to aestivate in caves in the Australian Alps, a distance of up to 1,800 miles (almost 3,000 km). In the fall, as temperatures cool and their hostplants begin to grow, they return north to breed.

T R O P I C S

Use your smartphone to scan here and learn why Taiwan is known as the butterfly kingdom.

Moving Out

When seasonal changes give the signal, some species *migrate*, or change location. They may be avoiding cold winter temperatures, or avoiding the worst of a *monsoon* rain, or they may be moving to new breeding grounds as food plants start to grow. The most studied migratory butterfly is the North American Monarch. Organizations such as Monarch Watch and Journey North work with volunteers, including students, teachers, and researchers all over North America, to compile information on Monarch migration. They record when and where people report Monarch sightings during the main flight south in the fall and the spring flight north.

MONITORING MIGRATION

Scientists study migration patterns to learn more about the routes the insects take, the time a journey takes them, if weather patterns affect their route, and if there are changes in their path from year to year. One way to gather data is tagging. A tiny sticker, or tag, with a number code is attached to the Monarch's hindwing, and a careful record is made of when and where the butterfly was released. When anyone finds a monarch with a tag, the code as well as the date and place where the butterfly was seen can be reported.

TAG@KU.EDU
MONARCH WATCH
1-888-TAGGING
MMY 849

A tagged Monarch butterfly

BUTTERFLY COLLECTIONS

Museum butterfly collections are important resources for modern-day research. Scientists use the specimens to study *evolution* and geographical distribution and to help identify and describe new species. During Victorian times in Great Britain, butterfly collecting was a very popular hobby. Wealthy people gathered huge collections by hiring professional explorers to capture exotic specimens in far-off lands. Many of those private collections were donated to museums, where scientists have been able to study them.

Tools of the Lepidopterist

To catch butterflies and moths, lepidopterists use special tools, like the ones pictured here. Can you find a fine-mesh nylon net, binoculars, a camera, a hand lens, a notebook, collecting jars, glassine envelopes, a spreading board, and insect pins?

1. Staff at a butterfly farm place nets on trees to protect the feeding caterpillars from predators.

Farm Friends

Butterfly farms are generally found in tropical areas where butterflies can be raised all year round. They supply local and worldwide exhibits. Farming local butterfly species is a good way to protect and preserve the environment, because the caterpillars need to feed on native hostplants. In many areas, farmers can earn more money from raising butterflies for export to conservatories than they can from clearing land to grow agricultural crops.

2. The growing caterpillars are checked daily and are moved to new branches when they need new leaves.

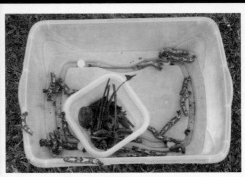

3. Staff collect caterpillars that are close to pupation and take them inside for extra protection.

4. Workers at a farm carefully wrap the chrysalides in soft tissue paper or cotton wool and pack them into boxes. Butterflies are transported in the chrysalis stage, as that is the safest point in the life cycle to ship them.

5. The boxes are sent by express delivery to arrive at the exhibit in one to three days. If shipped to a different country, usually both the farm and the exhibit must have permits to allow the box through customs inspections.

6. The chrysalides are unpacked at the conservatory and hung in special chambers, where the butterflies will emerge.

BUTTERFLY FARMING

Live butterfly exhibits and conservatories are a wonderful way to walk among butterflies. Conservatory conditions are usually as close as possible to the native habitats of the species displayed, so those showing tropical species are hot and steamy. Some exhibits may specialize in local species and raise their own caterpillars. Some include hundreds of species from all around the world and buy their butterflies from farms.

Butterfly conservatory at the American Museum of Natural History (AMNH)

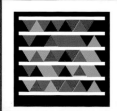

Use your smartphone to scan here and take a look inside a live butterfly conservatory.

What Is Being Done?

As people become more aware of the threats to butterfly and moth species, organizations have formed to lend a helping hand. The International Union for the Conservation of Nature lists all vulnerable, threatened, and endangered species in their Red Data Book. The Xerces Society, named after the Xerces Blue butterfly, develops conservation programs to protect invertebrates and their habitats worldwide.

Sometimes, if the population size falls too low, just protecting the places where butterflies live is not enough for the species to make a recovery. Managing and restoring habitats, by removing introduced plants and encouraging native plants to grow, is very important for conservation. Captive breeding programs, in which butterflies are raised in a lab and then released into the wild, are often included in a recovery plan and have helped species such as the Miami Blue in Florida.

Once found in sand dune habitats in the San Francisco Bay area, the Xerces Blue has not been seen since 1941. Unfortunately, it is probably extinct.

Did You Know?

You too can help conserve butterflies and moths. If you have space, cultivate a butterfly-friendly garden by planting native plants that attract butterflies. Find out if your local zoo or nature center needs volunteers to help with conservation programs.

Planting lupine, the hostplant for the Karner Blue, has helped reintroduce the butterfly to areas where it had disappeared.

Words to Know

abdomen: The third major body part, farthest from the head.

aestivation: To enter a period of inactivity during a dry or summer season.

antenna: A segmented sensory organ located on the head of an insect (plural antennae).

basking: A method of increasing body temperature, using the sun.

camouflage: A coloration and/or pattern that lets an organism blend in with its surrounding, hiding it from predators or prey.

carnivore: Meat-eating.

caterpillar: The second life stage of Lepidoptera.

chitin: A complex carbohydrate material that is a major component of an insect's exoskeleton.

chrysalis: The third life stage of a butterfly (plural, chrysalides). During this stage, the caterpillar changes into an adult butterfly.

cocoon: The silk casing produced by a moth larva for protecting the pupa during metamorphosis.

compound eye: An eye made up of many separate light-gathering units, or ommatidia.

conservation: The act of protecting the environment.

cryptic coloration: The combination of colors and patterns that allow an organism to blend in with the surroundings.

echolocation: Use of supersonic sound waves to determine the position of objects.

eclosion: The emergence of an adult butterfly or moth from its pupa.

endangered: An organism or ecosystem that is in danger of becoming extinct.

evolution: Changes in the genetic composition of a population over time, which are passed down through generations.

exoskeleton: An outer skeleton covering a body, as opposed to an internal skeleton.

extinct: No longer in existence.

forewings: The front pair of wings, closest to the head.

fossil: Any evidence of an organism of a past geological age, such as a skeleton or leaf imprint.

habitat: The area or environment where an organism or ecological community normally lives or occurs.

hemolymph: Insect body fluid, the equivalent of blood.

herbivore: Plant-eating animal.

hibernation: A period of inactivity through a cold or winter season.

hindwings: The rear pair of wings, farthest from the head.

hostplant: The particular food plant of a caterpillar.

instar: A growth stage between molts in an insect.

invertebrate: An animal without a spine.

larva: The second life stage of Lepidoptera (plural, larvae).

Lepidoptera: The order, or group, of insects that includes butterflies and moths.

metamorphosis: A change in form during development.

migrate: The process of changing location, as done by all, or a large percentage of a population.

mimicry: A physical resemblance between species that is beneficial to one or both of the species.

molting: Shedding of the exoskeleton to allow the insect to grow.

monsoon: A seasonal, heavy rainfall.

nectar: A sugar-rich liquid produced by flowers.

ommatidium: A single unit of a compound eye (plural ommatidia).

osmeterium: A brightly colored, smell-emitting organ, used by Swallowtail caterpillars for defense.

palps: A pair of sensory appendages found on either side of the proboscis.

pheromone: A chemical or scent, released primarily to attract a mate.

pollinators: Animals that move pollen from one flower to another, causing the plant to be fertilized and produce fruit.

predator: An animal that lives by hunting and eating other animals.

proboscis: The straw-like mouthpart through which adult Lepidoptera take in fluids (plural, proboscises).

prolegs: The fleshy legs on the abdominal segments of caterpillars.

pupa: The third life stage of Lepidoptera (plural pupae), during which metamorphosis into an adult occurs.

sexual dimorphism: Physical differences between males and females of the same species.

spiracles: Tiny openings along the side of an insect's thorax and abdomen that allow air to enter and leave the body.

tactile setae: Moveable hairlike structures that sense touch (singular, seta).

thorax: The second major body division of an insect, located just behind the head, where the legs and wings are attached.

tropics: An area parallel to the equator, located between the Tropic of Cancer and the Tropic of Capricorn.

Use your smartphone to scan here and see photos of many different butterflies.

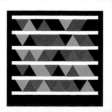

Did You Know?

The oldest Lepidoptera fossil is a primitive moth found in England, estimated to be 190 million years old. This means moths were alive at the time of the dinosaurs in the Jurassic period. Butterflies evolved from moths and have only been around for about 48 million years.

Specimen Specifics

A specimen is most useful if it has all the important information kept with it, such as when it was collected, in which country and specific locality, and the name of the person who caught it. This information is kept on a label attached to the pin below the butterfly or moth, along with another label with the name of the species. Keeping accurate, detailed records is important for any serious collection.

False Acraea in the AMNH collection

The American Museum of Natural History's Lepidoptera collection contains 3.5 million specimens! The earliest were collected about 200 years ago.

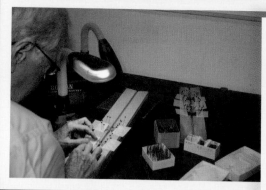

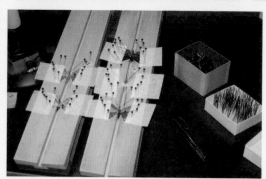

A specimen preparator pins moths on a spreading board for study

Lepidopterists at Work

Modern-day lepidopterists still collect and prepare specimens for study, but now they also use additional technology, such as scanning electron microscopes and DNA sequencing, to understand the biology and relationships of butterflies and moths.

Collecting moths

Night Shift

Because most moths fly at night, collecting them and learning more about them can be difficult. Luckily, moths are attracted to lights, so this is a good way to find them. Scientists who want to study moths in remote areas take lights out with them, and set them up next to a large white sheet to give the moths a place to land.

Bibliography

Bänziger, H. 1990. "Moths with a taste for tears: Insects that live off the tears of mammals find the secretions a tasty and nutritious food. The moths wisely favour mild-mannered herbivores as their victims." *New Scientist*. 1744:48–51.

Daniels, J. C. & Sanchez, S. J. 2006. "Blues' Revival: Can a Change in Diet—and a Little Laboratory Assistance—Help a Florida Butterfly Escape Extinction." *Natural History*. October:26–28.

Davies, H. & Butler, C. A. 2008. *Do Butterflies Bite? Fascinating Answers to Questions about Butterflies and Moths*. New Jersey: Rutgers University Press.

DeVries, P. J. 1987. *The Butterflies of Costa Rica and their Natural History, Vol. I: Papilionidae, Pieridae, Nymphalidae*. New Brunswick, New Jersey: Princeton University Press.

Downes, J. A. 1973. "Lepidoptera feeding at puddle-margins, dung and carrion." *Journal of the Lepidopterist Society*. 27:89–99.

Hoy, R. R. 1992. "The Evolution of Hearing in Insects as an Adaptation to Predation by Bats." *The Evolutionary Biology of Hearing*. eds. D. B. Webster, R. R. Fay, & A. N. Popper. 115–129. New York: Springer.

Larsen, T. 1992. *The Butterflies of Kenya and Their Natural History*. New York: Oxford University Press.

Larsen, T. 1993. "Butterfly Mass Transit." *Natural History*. Vol. 102, Issue 6.

Rubinoff, D. & Haines, W. P. 2005. "Web-Spinning Caterpillar Stalks Snails." *Science*. 309:575.

Salmon, M. A. 2000. *The Aurelian Legacy: British Butterflies and their Collectors*. Berkeley and Los Angeles: University of California Press.

Schappert, P. 2000. *A World for Butterflies: Their Lives, Behavior and Future*. Buffalo, NY: Firefly Books.

Scoble, M. J. 1992. *The Lepidoptera: Form, Function and Diversity*. London: Oxford University Press.

Scott, J. A. 1986. *The Butterflies of North America: A Natural History and Field Guide*. Stanford, California, Stanford University Press.

Shapiro, A. 2005. "Painted Lady Butterflies on the Wing." On the Web site UC Davis News and Information. http://www.news.ucdavis.edu/search/news_detail.lasso?id=7324. Accessed January 8, 2010.

Wagner, D. L. 2005. *Caterpillars of Eastern North America*. Princeton, New Jersey: Princeton University Press.

Find Out More

WEB SITES:
American Museum of Natural History:
The Butterfly Conservatory
http://www.amnh.org/exhibitions/butterflies/
Ology: Biodiversity
http://www.amnh.org/ology/index.php?channel=biodiversity
Ology: Zoology
http://www.amnh.org/ology/index.php?channel=zoology#channel

General Information and Species Identification:
http://www.butterfliesandmoths.org/
http://www.lepsoc.org/index.php
http://www.naba.org/
http://www.ukbutterflies.co.uk/index.php
http://www.ukleps.org/

Migration:
http://www.learner.org/jnorth/
http://www.monarchprogram.org/index.htm
http://www.monarchwatch.org/

Conservation:
http://www.butterfly-conservation.org/
http://www.butterflyrecovery.org/about/
http://www.xerces.org/
http://www.iucnredlist.org/

BOOKS:
Bartlett Wright, A. 1993. *Peterson First Guide to Caterpillars*. Boston: Houghton Mifflin.

Burris, J., and W. Richards. 2006. *The Life Cycles of Butterflies*. North Adams: Storey Publishing.

Carter, D. 1992. *Eyewitness Handbook to Butterflies and Moths*. London: DK Publishing.

Grace, E. S. 1997. *The World of the Monarch Butterfly*. San Francisco: Sierra Club.

Hofmann, H., and T. Marktanner. 2001. *Collins Nature Guides: Butterflies and Moths of Britain and Europe*. London: HarperCollins.

Opler, P. 1998. *Peterson First Guides: Butterflies and Moths*. Boston: Houghton Mifflin.

Whalley, P. 1988. *Eyewitness Books: Butterfly and Moth*. New York: Dorling Kindersley.

Index

If you don't have a smartphone, use these URLs to link up with related information on butterflies, from the American Museum of Natural History:

Page 36:
http://www.amnh.org/insidebooks/butterflykingdom

Page 40:
http://www.amnh.org/insidebooks/butterflycam

Page 42:
http://www.amnh.org/insidebooks/butterflypics